A New True Book

REINDEER

By Emilie U. Lepthien

 CHILDRENS PRESS®
CHICAGO

Reindeer pulling a sled

To Christopher and Clayton Capton

Project Editor: Fran Dyra
Design: Margrit Fiddle

Library of Congress Cataloging-in-Publication Data

Lepthien, Emilie U. (Emilie Utteg)
   Reindeer / by Emilie U. Lepthien.
       p.   cm.–(A New true book)
   Includes index.
   ISBN 0-516-01059-X
   1.   Reindeer–Juvenile literature.
2.   Caribou–Juvenile literature.   [1.   Reindeer.
2.   Caribou.]   I.   Title.
QL737.U55L46   1994
599.73'57–dc20   93-3442
                                                       CIP
                                                         AC

PHOTO CREDITS
© Bryan and Cherry Alexander Photography–
Cover, 10, 14, 18, 22, 25, 28, 29 (2 photos),
33, 35
© Erwin and Peggy Bauer–39
The Bettmann Archive–5
Dembinsky Photo Associates–© M. L.
Dembinsky, Jr., 19
© Hannu Hautala–13, 15, 26, 43, 45
© Emilie Lepthien–21, 42
North Wind Picture Archives–7
Photri–36 (bottom)
Root Resources–© Ben Goldstein, 23
© Bob & Ira Spring–8, 27
Tom Stack & Associates–© Warren & Genny
Garst, 31
Tony Stone Images–© Mittet Foto, 30; © Don
Smetzer, 32
SuperStock International, Inc.–11; © Alvis
Upitis, 9; © Niklas Deak, 16
Valan–© Joseph R. Pearce, 12 (left);
© Stephen J. Krasemann, 12 (right), 36 (top);
© Johnny Johnson, 40
Visuals Unlimited–© N. Pecnik, 2; © Will
Troyer, 38
Map–27
COVER: Lapp woman with reindeer

TABLE OF CONTENTS

Sinterklaas . . . 4

Reindeer and Caribou . . . 9

Reindeer Bodies . . . 13

Antlers . . . 15

Diet . . . 18

Special Hooves . . . 20

Summer and Winter Homes . . . 22

Mating and Calving . . . 24

Lapps and Their Reindeer . . . 27

Migration . . . 33

North American Caribou . . . 37

Imported Reindeer . . . 41

Hazards . . . 43

Santa Claus Land . . . 44

Words You Should Know . . . 46

Index . . . 47

SINTERKLAAS

At Christmas, we think of Santa Claus and his eight reindeer flying around the world. But why reindeer?

The story begins in Europe, where Saint Nicholas was a symbol for gift giving at Christmastime. The Dutch were especially fond of Saint Nicholas.

The children of Dutch settlers in North America called him *Sinterklaas*. To

This painting shows Saint Nicholas riding through the streets giving gifts to Dutch children.

English-speaking children, this sounded like "Santa Klaus." Soon, pictures appeared of Santa as a tall, thin man riding a white horse.

Then, in the early 1800s, a man named Clement Moore wrote a poem that began "'Twas the night before Christmas." In the poem, Santa Claus traveled in a sleigh pulled by eight tiny reindeer.

Forty years later, Thomas Nast, an American cartoonist, drew a big, jolly Santa Claus with a white

Thomas Nast's drawing shows a merry old Santa Claus carrying presents for children.

beard. All year long he made toys and delivered them at Christmas. He also drove a sleigh pulled by eight reindeer.

7

Reindeer are still used to pull sleighs in Lapland.

The poem and pictures may have been based on the Lapp people of northern Scandinavia. Their sleighs were pulled by reindeer. And Santa Claus was said to live in the frigid north.

Reindeer are the world's only domesticated deer.

REINDEER AND CARIBOU

Reindeer belong to the deer family. The wild reindeer of North America are called caribou. The scientific name for both reindeer and caribou is *Rangifer tarandus*.

Reindeer are good swimmers. They often cross rivers as they migrate.

Reindeer are native to northern Europe and Asia. They migrate across the northern parts of Norway, Sweden, Finland, and Siberia. At one time, reindeer probably roamed throughout

These drawings of reindeer were made by Stone Age people in a cave in France.

Europe. Beautiful paintings of reindeer and other animals have been found in caves in France and Spain. The artists lived during the Old Stone Age, at least 25,000 years ago. Reindeer were likely an excellent source of food for these Stone Age hunters.

The woodland caribou (above) and the barren ground caribou (right) live in Canada and Alaska.

Two kinds of caribou are native to North America. The barren ground caribou lives in Alaska and northern Canada. The woodland caribou is found in southeastern Canada and Newfoundland.

A male reindeer

REINDEER BODIES

Male reindeer, or bulls, stand 3 to 4 feet (90 to 120 cm) tall at the shoulder. They weigh up to 400 pounds (180 kg). The females, or cows, are smaller.

Reindeer have thick coats. Their fur is brown with white patches on the neck, rump, and feet. Their underfur is thick and woolly.

Their nose, or muzzle, has a thick coat of hair to protect it when the animal digs in the snow for food.

Reindeer digging in the snow for plants to eat. The hardy lichen plants of the Arctic grow under the snow in winter.

The male reindeer shown here has much larger antlers than the female.

ANTLERS

Both male and female reindeer have antlers. The female has smaller antlers than the male. Reindeer shed their antlers and grow new ones each year.

15

The brow antler grows forward and sticks out over the animal's muzzle.

When antlers begin to grow, they are covered with soft, furry skin called velvet. When the antlers are fully grown, the animal rubs off the velvety fur.

One branch of the

antlers is called the brow

antler. It sticks out over the animal's muzzle.

The male's antlers are shed in late fall or early winter. The females keep their antlers until March. New antlers begin to grow as soon as the old pair is shed.

The position of a male in the herd is determined by the size of its antlers. The male with the largest antlers is the most important animal.

In the summer, the tundra has plenty of grass and lichens for reindeer to eat.

DIET

During the summer, reindeer feed on grasses and the tender shoots of birch and willow trees. In winter they eat lichens and reindeer moss. Reindeer

18

Reindeer moss is the chief food of reindeer and caribou in the Arctic.

moss is actually a grayish-green lichen—a plant composed of an alga and a fungus.

Lichens have a high mineral content and provide nourishing food for the reindeer.

Reindeer herds move as they graze, so they do not wipe out vast areas of the slow-growing lichens.

SPECIAL HOOVES

Reindeer are ungulates—they have hooves. They use the sharp edges of their hooves to scrape snow and thin ice away from the lichens. If the ice is thick, they may not be able to break through it to the lichens. Then the animals may starve.

Reindeer hooves are large. In deep snow, they spread apart to help the animals walk. Reindeer also have dewclaws on their feet.

Reindeer have cloven hooves:
the hooves are divided into two large toes.

Their dewclaws help support them on the soft soil of the summer tundra.

When reindeer and caribou walk, their legs and ankles make a clicking sound. The clicking is caused by friction in an ankle tendon.

21

The tundra in summer

SUMMER AND WINTER HOMES

Reindeer spend their summers on the arctic tundra. In winter, they move south, where there are trees. Reindeer are bothered by mosquitoes and large flies. In late spring and early summer, they find a patch of snow and rest together. The insects do not bother them as much when they rest on the snow.

Reindeer rest on patches of snow to get away from biting insects.

MATING AND CALVING

Reindeer mate while they are migrating to their winter range. The mating, or rutting, season is in late August and early September. Adult bulls try to gather a group of five to twenty cows. They use their antlers in roaring fights with other males. The strongest bulls mate with the cows.

The cows and their calves from the previous

A reindeer
mother cleaning
her newborn
calf

year gather in the calving
area. There, new calves
are born. The older calves
must now leave their
mothers.

A reindeer calf takes its first steps
a few hours after it is born.

A newborn calf has two
small stubs of antlers
already growing on its
head. Two hours after birth
it can stand up and walk.
In only a few days, it can
travel as fast as its mother
on the migration.

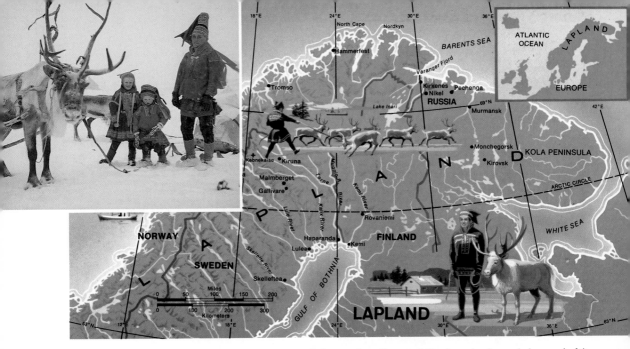

A Lapp family and their reindeer (above left).

LAPPS AND THEIR REINDEER

The area called Lapland lies in far northwest Europe. Lapland covers parts of Norway, Sweden, Finland, and Russia. It is named for the people who live there—the Lapps.

Reindeer herders live in tents at this winter camp.

For hundreds of years, the Lapps have lived by following reindeer herds. The reindeer provide the Lapps with meat and milk. Reindeer milk is four times richer in butterfat than cow's milk.

In the past, Lapp families lived in a tent called a *kota* while tending their herds. Today, the families stay in houses and herders use snowmobiles to follow their reindeer.

A Lapp settlement in Norway. An exhausted young reindeer (inset) gets a ride during the spring migration.

All of this Lapp girl's clothing is made from reindeer skins.

The Lapps use the reindeer in many ways. Reindeer hides are used to make tents, parkas, trousers, gloves, boots, and bedding. Sinews make thread for sewing. Bones and antlers are used to

A Lapp man wears traditional
reindeer-hide boots with curved toes.

make knives and other
tools. The ends of antlers
make good fishhooks.

The Lapps need the
reindeer. They sell lots of
reindeer skins. They also
sell cheese made from
reindeer milk. Reindeer

meat is sold to Japan and other countries.

Reindeer antlers, however, bring in the most money. They are cut into small pieces and then cooked with other ingredients. Asian men believe this mixture will restore their youth.

Asian woman buying reindeer antlers in a shop

Migrating reindeer move through a valley in Norway.

MIGRATION

Lapps do not drive their reindeer herds like ranchers drive their cattle. Instead, the Lapps follow the reindeer as they migrate. Despite hundreds of years of herding, the Lapps have been unable to breed out the reindeer's desire to travel from place to place.

For hundreds of years, reindeer pulled Lapp sleighs during migration. Nine or ten reindeer were harnessed in single file to pull a sleigh. Reindeer are strong. They can travel 18 miles (29 km) an hour pulling a sleigh with two men.

As pack animals, they can travel 40 miles (64 km) in a day carrying a 90-pound (41-kg) load

Reindeer pulling sleds on the spring migration in Siberia

while pulling a 450-pound (204 kg) load.

The reindeer's top speed is 32 miles (51 km) an hour. They can maintain a steady trot over a long distance.

Barren ground caribou (above). These caribou migrate
across great distances in North America (below).

NORTH AMERICAN CARIBOU

North American caribou live in the arctic tundra and the northern taiga forests.

Caribou are larger than reindeer. They measure up to 8 feet (2.4 m) long and stand 4 feet (1.2 m) high at the shoulder.

Barren ground caribou spend about four months of the year in migration.

They migrate to escape the summer heat and the spring insects. They winter in the taiga forests. In spring, they move to the tundra. The females give birth to their calves in long-established calving areas.

This barren ground caribou calf will soon join its mother on the migration.

Woodland caribou

Woodland caribou are slightly larger than barren ground caribou. They are also darker in color.

At one time, as many as two million caribou roamed across North America. But by the end of the 1800s,

Caribou bulls in winter in Denali National Park, Alaska

the big herds were gone. They were almost wiped out by hunters with rifles. Now the herds have been restored and the caribou population stands at about one million.

Alaska has about fifteen herds, with a total of 400,000 to 500,000 animals.

IMPORTED REINDEER

   Reindeer were imported from Siberia to Alaska between 1892 and 1902 following a famine. They were brought in to replace caribou that had been hunted almost to extinction because many Alaskan natives were starving. More than a million reindeer descended from these imported animals now live in western Alaska.

   The University of Alaska at Fairbanks' Large Animal

Caribou, reinbou, and carideer all live together at the Large Animal Research Station in Fairbanks, Alaska.

Research Station of the Institute of Arctic Biology has crossbred reindeer and caribou. The result is carideer and reinbou. (The first half of the name is the male parent's.)

Some reindeer were imported to Iceland from Norway many years ago.

A car slows down for a herd of reindeer in Finland.

HAZARDS

In Finland, more than 4,000 reindeer are killed on roads each year. Predators— such as wolverines, wolves, lynxes, and bears—also kill many caribou.

SANTA CLAUS LAND

In 1984, Lapland was declared "Santa Claus Land." Santa Claus Village was built on the Arctic Circle. The Arctic Circle is an imaginary line around the Earth in the far north. A post office at Santa Claus Village receives the letters that children all over the world send to Santa Claus.

The reindeer in Lapland live under incredibly harsh

arctic conditions. They are strong and graceful, the perfect choice for Santa Claus—and almost a legend themselves.

WORDS YOU SHOULD KNOW

alga (AL • juh)–a tiny green plant

antlers (ANT • lerz)–bony, hornlike growths on the head of an animal

arctic (ARK • tik)–like the cold and icy region of the Earth around the North Pole

cartoonist (car • TOO • nist)–a person who draws amusing pictures

dewclaw (DOO • klaw)–a short toe on the inside of an animal's front foot

extinction (ex • TINK • shun)–the dying out of an entire species

fungus (FUNG • guss)–a plant that has no flowers or leaves and no green coloring

hazard (HAZ • erd)–a cause of danger

imported (im • POR • tid)–brought in from another place

lichen (LYE • kin)–a plant composed of an alga and a fungus living together

migrate (MY • grait)–to travel, usually for a long distance, to find better food or better weather conditions

mineral (MIN • ril)–a substance such as iron or calcium needed by the body in small amounts

native (NAY • tiv)–born in a place; belonging to a certain place

predator (PREH • dih • ter)–an animal that hunts other animals for food

scientific name (sy • en • TIF • ik NAYME)–a name, usually from the Latin language, given by scientists to a plant or an animal

settlers (SET • lerz)–people who come to a new country to establish farms or other homes

sinew (SIN • yoo)–another name for a tendon

Sinterklaas (SIN • ter • klahs)–the Dutch name for Santa Claus

sleigh (SLAY)–a cart with runners instead of wheels for traveling over snow; a sled

symbol (SIM • bil)–a thing that stands for something else or for an idea

taiga (TYE • ga)–The evergreen forest region south of the arctic tundra

tendon (TEN • dun)–a tough band of tissue that joins a muscle to a bone

tundra (TUN • dra)–a cold, treeless area where the vegetation consists of short grasses, mosses, and lichens

ungulates (UNG • gyoo • laits)–animals with hooves

INDEX

Alaska, 12, 41

alga, 19

antlers, 15-17, 24, 26, 30, 31, 32

Arctic Circle, 44

Asia, 10

barren ground caribou, 12, 37-38, 39

bears, 43

bedding, 30

birch trees, 18

bones, 30

boots, 30

bulls, 13, 24

calves, 24-25, 26, 38

Canada, 12

caribou, 9, 12, 21, 37-40, 41, 42, 43

carideer, 42

cave paintings, 11

cheese, 31

Christmas, 4, 7

clicking sound, 21

cows, 13, 24

deer family, 9

dewclaws, 20, 21

Dutch, 4

Europe, 4, 10, 11, 27

females, 13, 15, 17

Finland, 10, 27, 43

fishhooks, 31

flies, 23

food, 14, 18-19

France, 11

fungus, 19

fur, 14, 16

gloves, 30

grasses, 18

hooves, 20

hunters and hunting, 40, 41

Iceland, 42

Institute of Arctic Biology, 42

knives, 31

kota, 29

Large Animal Research Station, 41-42

Lapland, 27, 44

Lapp people, 8, 27, 28, 29, 30, 31, 33-34

lichens, 18, 19, 20

lynxes, 43
males, 13, 15, 17, 24
mating, 24
meat, 28, 31-32
migration, 10, 24, 26, 33-35, 37
milk, 28, 31
Moore, Clement, 6
mosquitoes, 22
muzzle, 14
Nast, Thomas, 6
Newfoundland, 12
North America, 4, 9, 12, 39
Norway, 10, 27, 42
nose, 14
Old Stone Age, 11
parkas, 30
poem, 6, 8
predators, 43
Rangifer tarandus, 9
reinbou, 42
reindeer, 4, 6, 7, 8, 9, 10, 11,
    13-35, 37, 41, 42, 43, 44
reindeer moss, 18-19
Russia, 27
Saint Nicholas, 4
Santa Claus, 4, 5, 6, 7, 8, 44, 45
Santa Claus Village, 44
Scandinavia, 8

Siberia, 10, 41
sinews, 30
Sinterklaas, 4
size of caribou, 37, 39
size of reindeer, 13
sleighs, 6, 7, 8, 34
snow, 20, 23
snowmobiles, 29
Spain, 11
speed of reindeer, 35
spring, 23, 38
summer, 21, 22, 23, 38
Sweden, 10, 27
tendon, 21
tents, 29, 30
taiga forest, 37, 38
trees, 22
trousers, 30
tundra, 21, 22, 37, 38
ungulates, 20
University of Alaska at
    Fairbanks, 41-42
velvet, 16
willow trees, 18
winter, 20, 22
wolverines, 43
wolves, 43
woodland caribou, 12, 39

About the Author

Emilie U. Lepthien received her BA and MS degrees and certificate in school administration from Northwestern University. She taught upper-grade science and social studies, wrote and narrated science programs for the Chicago Public Schools' station WBEZ, and was principal in Chicago, Illinois, for twenty years. She received the American Educator's Medal from Freedoms Foundation.

She is a member of Delta Kappa Gamma Society International, Chicago Principals' Association, Illinois Women's Press Association, National Federation of Press Women, and AAUW.

She has written books in the Enchantment of the World, New True Books, and America the Beautiful series.